MEMORIES AND ELEPHANTS

MEMORIES AND ELEPHANTS

THE ART OF CASUAL RACISM

Meaghan Katrak Harris

A catalogue record for this book is available from the National Library of Australia.

Trade Paperback ISBN: 978-0-6452626-1-2
eBook ISBN: 978-0-6452626-2-9

Cover design by Nada Backovic
Internal design by Nicola Matthews
Edited by Georgia Jordan
Cover image by iStock

Print information available on the last page.

We at The Kind Press acknowledge that Aboriginal and Torres Strait Islander peoples are the Traditional Custodians and the first storytellers of the lands on which we live and work; and we pay our respects to Elders past and present.

THE
KIND
PRESS

www.thekindpress.com

For my Family

of Blood and of Life

I would like to acknowledge the Traditional Custodians of the Land and acknowledge sovereignty was never ceded. I pay my respects to Elders, Past, Present and Emerging.

Always was, always will be Aboriginal Land.

Contents

A preface

This collection of essays is titled *Memories and Elephants*. You thought it was a bit of an 'If you know, you know' title. Everyone back home knows Creedence Clearwater Revival. Everyone knows 'Lookin' Out my Back Door'.

You started writing these essays after thinking, *Someone would write about that*, and finally deciding, *You are someone. You should write about that.*

As you neared completion of the collection and started thinking about titles, it came to you.

Memories and Elephants.

Perfect. Lots of memories. Perhaps addressing the odd Elephant in the Room.

Doo, doo, doo, lookin', out my back door.

Except you'd got it wrong. The lyrics are actually *tambourines and elephants*.

You know you all used to sing 'memories and

elephants' back home, before Google could sort that stuff out instantly. You remember playing the song over and over one Christmas, arguing the toss on the lyrics with your partner and brother. You were sure it was 'memories' then, and you had stuck to it.

You thought about the title again.

Even better, you decided. These essays are your stories and your truth. Other people will have different perspectives. Other people will have different memories.

Memories and Elephants.

WITH
APOLOGIES TO
HELEN
GARNER
AND
THANKS TO
ELIZABETH
GILBERT

You didn't know why this compulsion to write had hit you now, but it had sideswiped you in a way that left you reeling, breathless.

You had always liked the idea of writing, but this was different. It'd come like a wave of urgency, leaving you dizzy and discombobulated.

Like the first thrill of a love affair, it was all you could think about.

Having been employed in the university world for the past decade, you had written academic things, of course, a few texts and articles. Now, your head was buzzing with stories—your stories—and you felt compelled to get them down.

But why now, this desire to move beyond academia and write? Was this about getting older, about making sense of your own life, your own history? *Hardly contemplation time with two kids still at school,* you thought, sitting in the car line, waiting for the school bell to go and the littlest one to come rushing out, curls flying.

You felt a sense of urgency to read as well, essays or memoir-based stories in particular. Thank goodness; it made you feel less absorbed in your own stories, which played on a constant loop in your head.

You had specific authors in mind who resonated, whose thoughts and ideas had lodged in your mind, resurfacing now and then in your thoughts, and you were drawn back to them.

You'd read Helen Garner over the years. Who hasn't? An icon in Australian literature who writes non-fiction and semi-autobiographically, her prolific career spanning four decades.

You remembered discussing her with a friend—having both just read, and loved, one of her books—years ago.

You remembered saying critically to your friend, 'Yes, but I read this article on how she draws from *everything* … I mean, imagine having her at the Christmas table, taking it all down!'

It was Garner's own ruthless self-critique that you

were in awe of, her great skill of including herself in her unflinching social commentary. Now you were desperate to read everything she had 'taken down' with an obsessive interest. Now you were riveted by the honest elegance of her writing. You knew now your criticism had been born of enviousness of her ability to direct her unflinching gaze onto her own character.

You remembered a quote about Joan Didion, saying 'Joan writes to know what she thinks.' *Is that what it's all about?* you wondered. *Working out what you think?*

You rushed to a local bookshop.

'Joan Didion?' replied the matron behind the counter. 'Which book?'

'Oh, what do you have?' you asked hopefully.

'Well, none,' she replied, peering over her glasses. *'There is nothing new.'*

For some reason, that annoyed you greatly. The thought that a book has to be new to be of value—in a bookshop, no less.

You went home and got online. Within twenty-four hours, you had three Joan Didion and four Helen Garner texts on your bedside table, one of Didion's having been first published in 1968—so no, not new.

You were very cognisant of the fact you could, in fact, afford to order seven books at once. This hadn't always been the case and you felt fortunate.

You were in the thrall of these texts, the academic paper you were working on languishing in Google Docs.

You started making deals with yourself. Work on the paper for four hours, then you can write something. Edit today's work on the paper and you can read something else.

You headed to the school car line earlier and earlier, telling yourself you'd never get a spot if you didn't, and you'd have to queue for ages. You sat in the sun and read, without guilt, waiting for the school bell.

You've always been a reader, but you hadn't read with this intensity for years.

'Do you think *everyone* thinks they can write?' you asked your husband.

'Everyone like us,' he replied nonchalantly.

You wondered what he meant by *us*, your life experiences having been so very different. Him with his classical education. You who didn't finish year 9 at Robinvale High. You had gone on to earn bachelor, master's and PhD degrees, but still, you'd had to check if it was a 'classic' or 'classical' education—the kind you didn't have.

'Should I do a course? A master's in creative writing?' You felt embarrassed, self-indulgent, trying to convey the enormity of this feeling, of this urgency, to him.

'I think you should just write, Meagh,' he answered. *Just write.*

You'd moved on to Garner's movies. Your husband came in while you were watching.

'*Monkey Grip?*' he asked.

You thought it was his copy you first read, twenty-five years ago.

He watched as Nora's (played by Noni Hazlehurst) young daughter, Gracie (played by Garner's actual daughter, Alice), was getting some money for a school excursion from her mother's purse while her mother stirred, having slept in with her new lover.

'Those were the days,' your husband quipped. 'When the kids got themselves ready for school while you laid in bed with your lover.'

'It doesn't seem to have done Alice Garner any harm,'

you snapped. 'She's a successful classical musician and actor, has a PhD in history and lives next door to her mother with her husband and three kids.'

Your husband knew you well enough to not be surprised or alarmed by your sudden expertise in all matters Garner.

You extended your Australian reading obsession to Julia Baird's new text *Phosphorescence*, a book that grabbed you intensely. A perfect mix of memoir, academic and literary.

Before you finished the first chapters, you'd ordered a copy for two friends, one of whom had lost a dear friend to cancer and one who was in COVID-19 lockdown.

As you stretched out the final chapters (you didn't want it to end), Baird talked of her introduction to Helen Garner's work twenty years ago, of devouring her work in a fever. You might have been late to the party, but you felt in good company.

You remembered the Elizabeth Gilbert book you read a few years ago, *Big Magic*—all about creativity. Gilbert is an award-winning fiction and non-fiction writer who is probably most well known for her bestseller *Eat, Pray,*

Love. This is her story of self-discovery after her divorce that takes her on a spiritual odyssey through Italy, Bali and India. It was also made into a blockbuster movie.

Gilbert herself doesn't consider it her best work, but is wonderfully philosophical about the craft of writing and the sometimes-arbitrary nature of success. You had read *Big Magic* a few years ago, and enjoyed it, but it hadn't galvanised you into action in any way, creatively. You felt a sudden compulsion to read it again and rushed to get it off the shelf.

This time it knocked your socks off.

Gilbert describes:

> The hairs on the back of my neck stood up for an instant, and I felt a little sick, a little dizzy. I felt like I was falling in love, or had just heard alarming news, or was looking over a precipice to something beautiful and mesmerising, but dangerous.
>
> I'd experienced these symptoms before, so I knew immediately what was going on ... I believe I can confidently call it by its name: inspiration.

This explained exactly what you had been feeling in tangible waves, and you ploughed through the book. You felt almost panic-stricken, as though this thing would pass you by if you didn't grab it now, get hold of it, whatever it was. Thankfully, Gilbert follows this recognition of 'The Magic' with the sound advice of 'Do the Work'. Inspiration will come and go, just keep doing the work.

She talks about finding the pleasure and fun in the craft, and isn't a fan of the tortured-artist trope. You didn't feel tortured at all. You felt happy and free and light.

You spontaneously started taking notes all the time—ideas, phrases, thoughts. You had read in more than one memoir-inspired essay that this is what writers do, and wondered why you hadn't realised that. The idea of inspiration and how it strikes and surrounds you, like you were in on it for the first time.

On Instagram, author Trent Dalton posted ideas and visual inspiration for this latest novel straight from his mood wall—or 'fever wall', as he called it. Dalton explained: 'Because I think you have to be a little feverish with the story you love when you're writing it, a little ill with it.' You knew that feverish, punch-drunk-in-love and slightly obsessed feeling.

You updated your husband: 'Liz Gilbert says that most writers get rejected two hundred times on average before they're published ... I've only got about twelve stories in me!'

'Just write, Meagh, just write.'

THE ART OF
CASUAL RACISM

The Mildura Show, early 1990s

Mildura on the Murray River. The Heart of Sunraysia in North West Victoria. An artificial 'oasis' in the harsh Mallee landscape, rendered unnaturally green and fertile thanks to the Canadian Chaffey Brothers and the irrigation system they built in the late 1800s. Mildura would go on to be known as Australia's food bowl.

The politics of water and the looming disaster ahead for the Murray River hadn't yet reached you in the early 1990s. Mildura was considered a well-laid-out, attractive regional 'city'. Wide, green nature strips and tree-lined avenues. Apparently Australian gardening icon Kevin Heinz had visited sometime in the seventies or eighties and was asked what would grow well here. 'Bottlebrush,' it is said he replied, offhandedly. He was taken at his word and street after street was now a frenzy of *Callistemon*, evergreen native shrubs whose red flower spikes form the exact shape of a bottlebrush.

Held annually, the Mildura Show is your typical country show. Noise and crowds, sideshows and rides that look glitzy and exciting at night and a bit tired and sad during the day, if you look too closely. Thrilling nonetheless for country kids and still considered a local highlight.

This particular year you and your partner had loaded the three kids into the beige Holden Commodore and driven ninety kilometres from your hometown of Robinvale to attend the show, along with at least half the community. You were a young mum, young enough that over thirty-five years later you understand that your daughter's birth created somewhat of a stir in sectors in your small hometown. That and your partner's Aboriginality.

You can remember when you got it, the Commodore. Your newest car yet. Current Shape, a real shift within the eighties and nineties when cars suddenly were smaller, boxier and looked more modern. It was a Big Deal to you and your partner, purchased during the days when you made an appointment with the local bank manager, and he looked at your job, looked at you, and decided if you were in stable employment and of good enough character to be given a loan to buy a car. Apparently, you both were. And your dad guaranteed it, so there was that too.

You remember when your partner walked in to pay for petrol not long after buying the Commodore (second hand, by the way), and a local asked him, 'Whose car?'

'Mine,' said your partner.

'Jeez,' said the local, 'youse are getting better cars than us now.' *Youse* of course meaning Aboriginal people, *us* being him, the white man who, somehow by his way of thinking, should have a better car by virtue of his whiteness. You remember you and your partner shaking your heads at the local's ignorance.

Robinvale (population 1600), was a young town, even by the metrics of the colonisers, the invaders. Less than a century old. A soldier settlement. Parcels of land called 'blocks' had been carved up and distributed to returned soldiers after the Second World War by the Government to grow grapes and citrus. The surrounding roads were later named after the battlegrounds these soldiers had returned from: Damascus Road, Crete Road, Malaya Road. A neat little town proud of its soldier settlement beginnings.

In the fiftieth-anniversary book *Robinvale ... the first fifty years*, published in the 1970s, the town's historians document their prideful pioneer story. In this story, Aboriginal people were not present here in Robinvale prior to the township's establishment. The historians' version conveniently tells us Aboriginal people arrived in the area around the same time as the white settlers. Millenia of Aboriginal history would dispute that, and tell us that Aboriginal people always lived along the River. However, the historical committee felt confident enough to republish that same spiel thirty years later in the 2000s, for the eightieth anniversary—somewhat depleted and less excited celebrations. There aren't many original soldier settlers left now, or original family blocks. Aboriginal People are still here.

But on this day, the decision was what to do first at the Mildura Show. You and your partner decided to take the kids to the farm displays. They were probably more interested in the rides and showbags, but you two young parents did the Right Thing and headed to the agricultural show.

You were pushing the pram with the littlest baby boy, his primary-school-aged sister holding on, and the two-year-old being carried by their dad. You walked into the shed and started the procession around to look at the livestock. Sheep, definitely. Cows? Probably, you can't remember now.

It certainly smelled like a farm. All hay, dust, manure, the sharp stench that catches your nostrils. You grew up a 'townie' but were enough of a country girl that the farm display held no novelty for you.

An older farmer, very much looking the part in his beaten Akubra hat, was sitting in front of the sheep pens. (Now, in your mind's eye he was sitting on a hay bale, but that would be too clichéd. It was probably an aluminium fold-up chair.) You approached; kids interested, excited, your open-faced, open-hearted daughter smiling, your partner ready for a yarn (he loved a yarn, and people loved yarning with him). The farmer spoke loudly, to no one in particular, yet particularly to you. You were the only ones there.

'Have you heard about MABO?' he boomed, then quickly answered his own question. 'It stands for

"Money Available; Blacks Only".' It hung in the air, this statement. Heavy, hovering. For a second you weren't sure where it would land.

The Mabo Case had been big in the news—Eddie Mabo's decade-long struggle for the Meriam People of the Murray Islands in the Torres Strait to be recognised as Traditional Owners of their Lands. This significant case challenged the existing Australian legal system's assumption of terra nullius, or empty land, and was being followed and celebrated keenly in the Aboriginal community while unearthing a barely concealed racist vein in the white.

You and your partner looked at each other. You weren't shocked, nor frightened, more … *Here we go* …

'Let's go,' one of you said. (You can't remember which.) You kept walking. Not today. That day the statement was stepped over, kicked to the side and given no space.

'We just wanted to show the kids the animals,' you said to the farmer as you passed, hoping to shame him. He wouldn't return your gaze. You headed back to Side Show Alley. The Black Man, the White Woman and their Three Brown Kids.

Something may have been muttered between you about what exactly he could do, that farmer, with his poxy sheep.

Robinvale 1990s

You were sitting in the car in front of Fishers, the local supermarket. It must have been Christmas. You know this because your older brother was in the passenger seat next to you and it was a stinking hot day. He was home from Melbourne to visit, as he always did.

You two are very close even though he left for boarding school when you were eight or nine. At the time your auntie had said to your mum and dad that they were 'educating him above his station'. It didn't seem to have done him any harm.

He was your link to the Bigger World, in many ways. He bought you books, CDs and cool T-shirts. He'd studied law and history and worked for Native Title. An intellectual who can scull a beer, kick a footy and throw a punch, if need be. He is the Rock Star of your family.

There was a tap on the window and standing there was a White Lady. Pastel blouse? Tick. Popped collar? Tick. Pearl studs? Tick. Puffed up with her own sense of entitlement? Tick, tick, tick.

She was tapping on the glass and you wound the window down. 'Are you the Harris girl?' she asked. 'The one married to an Aborigine?' Did she notice the sharp intake of breath from you and your brother? You doubted it.

'Yes,' you said. 'My name is Meaghan.' Even in your shock, you tried to humanise this exchange.

'I want to talk to you,' she said. 'I'm so worried about my daughter.'

You knew who she was, this woman. You knew who her daughter was. You knew where this was going. Her daughter was going out with an Aboriginal boy. Obviously creating a Stir in her family.

'My daughter is going out with …' she began.

'I know,' you responded, cutting her off. 'He's a nice boy.' She looked at you imploringly, obviously wanting more from you. You didn't know what.

'His family are good people,' you said. 'Very well respected.'

'But,' she lamented, 'he hasn't even got a car.'

The rest of this awkward exchange is a bit of a blur. You remember trying to convey your thoughts about good character being more important maybe? About their youth, there being time for establishing a job, a life, stuff? Your brother was aghast, bristling in the seat next to you.

The White Lady departed, with a pained expression that told you whatever she had wanted from you remained unfulfilled. What *had* she wanted from you? Not, it seems, reassurance of the character of the boy, or his family. You and your brother looked at each other. *You couldn't make this shit up*, you thought.

Thirty-odd years later, you think about the boy in question. He'd be a middle-aged man now. You look up his profile on Facebook. He looks good, standing next to his shiny car.

Mildura mid 2000s

Life went on with the big dramatic changes that crashed through your world and at times seemed to cause irreparable damage, but this now just felt like the ebb and flow of life. Marriages had come and gone, and come. You lived in Mildura now, right in Bottlebrush Central. Family had extended and blended, as they do, in multiple directions. New jobs, new home, new chapters.

You were working at the largest local service provider, managing family services programs.

You were walking in the sunshine one day, toward the local park, enjoying your new neighbourhood. An older man was approaching, obviously walking his dog, who was unrestrained and bounding slightly ahead. The dog (a Labrador cross maybe?) came towards you. You're a bit scared of dogs so extended a friendly greeting to the dog, while eyeing the owner, hoping he would catch up soon.

'Come on, Rosie,' the man called to his dog as he came closer, crossing the grass towards you. He stopped and looked at you. 'Rosie doesn't like Blackfellas. Do you, Rosie?' he said, addressing the dog as he put on the leash.

Your chest tightened. You paused and looked around. *Who is this man? Does he just greet everyone on the street that way?* You know he must have seen your family. Your big brown sons. The gang of brown and black boys who hang out at your home too.

The statement felt menacing. You didn't look at the man, but addressed the dog. 'Don't you, Rosie?' you asked. Your voice sounded falsely lighthearted in your ears. 'Well, we can't be friends then.' You turned and kept walking.

The whole exchange, only a few minutes in length, left you feeling winded.

Robinvale 2010s

You were home to visit from Sydney, on break from your university lecturer job that you had secured soon after completing your PhD. Life in Sydney was different, but rich in its own way. Gathering at your parent's place in Robinvale; kids, grandkids, your folk's great-grandkids—it's always good to be home.

One of your sons had driven down from Mildura and was relaying to you how he was stopped by the police driving down the main street of Robinvale. Well, the only street really.

Licence and registration were checked and in order.

'Whose car?' he was asked by the policeman, referring to his new (second hand) Holden Commodore.

'Mine,' he replied.

'Where'd you get it?' asked the policeman.

'I bought it.'

'How?'

'With money. I've been working since I was seventeen.'

'Youse are getting better cars than us,' replied the policeman, who sent him on his way.

Sydney 2021

It was your usual midweek dinner catch up with your daughter's family. Life was busier and fuller since they had made the move to the city too. Over a big, chaotic meal, you shared all the news. Your daughter Leshae had started a new job and was telling the story of a greeting from a colleague.

'Most importantly,' they had said to her before any

other introductions were made, 'what do you like to be called—Aboriginal or Indigenous?'

'Leshae is fine,' she'd responded wryly.

This I know is true

These exchanges of so-called casual racism are so frequent and flippant that they speak volumes about the psyche of white Australia. People are seen, judged and categorised with breathtaking ease.

Back home you felt part of the Aboriginal community you lived in. Much more so than the white community, if you had to delineate between the two. Of course, they intersected and the townsfolk would have many examples of how integrated the town was, in lots of ways. On the surface. On the football field.

Back home, back then, you were so confident in your place. The confidence born from love and acceptance from within the Community. Your position felt clearer to you, unquestioned, before community morphed into work and you realised that your white self might be Taking Up Too Much Space. That you might be

Overconfident in your place. The kind of unquestioning confidence that can be born from (yet unrecognised) white privilege itself.

This would, over the years, play out with great complexity for you internally. There's an intricacy to the insider/outsider dance that is hard to get right. Too many steps forward or too many back? You still feel the pain of it, the weight of it, the joy of it.

You know now, we are all more than one story.

SMALL TOWN STORY

.

They say the good thing about small towns is everybody knows you. They say the bad thing about small towns is everybody knows you.

You felt the weight of both of these truths in your life, in your small town.

It's true, however, that as a very young mum you felt a certain protection, a certain safety in being known, of your family being known. Of being 'someone' in this place.

Robinvale mid 1980s

—————————————

You'd taken your daughter to the doctor because she had a runny nose and a cough. She must have been about one year old, toddling around. The local doctor who knew you was away, and in his place was a locum from out of town.

He seemed kind and thorough; he examined your daughter, in her pretty dress, bow in her hair and glittery plastic sandals. 'It's nothing serious,' he reassured, but prescribed an antibiotic as was the norm then, back in the 1980s.

The next day, there was a knock at the door.

You were renting this house, owned by an older Italian man. An old housing-commission fibro place. You had decorated it nicely, you thought. Covered the old benchtops with self-adhesive contact of a geometric design that was fashionable at the time. A hand-me-down lounge suite and dining table were squeezed into the small open-plan space. Lots of photos on the walls.

It was the first house you and your partner lived in together, with your daughter. You had rented two flats before this, moving from a one bedroom to a two, and then upgrading to this place.

You'll move to a housing-commission house soon, before buying your own little home by the time you're twenty-one.

A short, stout woman with red hair was standing on the doorstep. She introduced herself brusquely, efficiently. She was from the Child Protection Office in Mildura, she told you, and had come to check on your little girl.

'Can I come in?' she asked.

You don't remember being worried or nervous at all, young and confident as you were.

'Sure,' you invited her in and offered her a cup of coffee.

She explained that the doctor had called Child Protection after your appointment requesting they visit you.

'But why?' you asked. 'She's only got a runny nose.'

'It's because you are so young,' she said.

Your little girl was grasping around your legs, wanting to be picked up, while you made the coffee.

'She seems demanding,' the Child Protection worker commented, and you knew she was sizing you up.

'No, not really,' you said. 'She's just a bit sick, which is why I took her to the doctor.'

She looked around the house, and asked if she could see your daughter's room.

'Sure,' you said.

All the rooms in the house opened off the living area,

so it didn't take long. She seemed satisfied with your daughter's bright room, with the doona with clowns on it and matching curtains your mum had made.

She asked if you had support. You had lots, you told her. Your partner, your parents, your partners' parents. She seemed happy enough with this and off she went.

Your mum and dad were on holidays, driving around Australia, and they rang a few times a week. When Mum called, you told her about the visit. She seemed worried and asked lots of questions about what was said.

You know now how Mum must have worried, away on holidays when this happened. You now wonder how it might have played out differently, this visit, if you hadn't been dressed up, both of you ready to go 'up the street' with friends. If her room hadn't been neat and bright. If the house had been a mess, as it could easily have been. How it might have been if you were shy and less responsive, or aggressive and uncooperative, or less able to advocate and present yourself confidently.

If you hadn't been white.

You know that now.

Early 1990s

You were at the hospital with the littlest boy, having been down the river fishing all day with your partner's family. He had croup, that honking, gasping cough that sounded too loud and harsh to be coming out of his little body. You had taken him before and had had to sleep in a steam tent with him until it eased.

You had rushed up this evening, leaving the two older kids home with their dad.

You knew this hospital well. You were born here. Your three kids were delivered by the same doctor that delivered you.

After the third baby, this little one, the doctor thought that was enough for you. 'Three is enough for Meagy,' he'd said to your dad over the bar at the Golf Club. 'That pregnancy was hard on her body.'

In the early 1990s, the hospital itself probably looked much as it did in the 1950s. All steel beds, polished linoleum floors and strong disinfectant smell.

You approached the sister in charge, as you still called them then. She was new and she didn't know you at all. You told her you were worried about your baby; he had croup and he'd had it before—

Before you finished, she cut you off. 'Take a seat,' she snapped, looking you up and down, standing imposingly in her starched uniform.

You were dressed casually, after a day at the river: bike shorts and a tie-dyed T-shirt. You sat down, soothing the baby, wishing someone would examine him. You were the only one there, there was no queue.

'Name?' she barked.

You told her.

Her demeanour changed a bit. 'Oh,' she said, 'are you related to Dorrie?'

'Yes,' you said. 'She's my grandmother.'

'Oh, I go to church with Dorrie!' she exclaimed. She looked at you and your little brown baby a bit differently then and began to examine him.

What if I wasn't someone's granddaughter? you wondered. *Would I be left sitting a bit longer while you made your disapproval felt?*

How different the experience was with those who knew you—like your relationship with Sister D, the maternal health nurse in your town when your kids were babies. Those were the days when the nurse would visit you at home quite regularly when the baby was born, and often keep visiting.

Sister was quite a fixture in your town. You knew she liked to visit you, especially as your friends would often be there with their babies too. That was okay; you all welcomed her, and she'd join you as you sat around drinking coffee.

Sister was quite a character, but her no-nonsense parenting advice probably influenced you more than you gave her credit for at the time. She was an advocate of breastfeeding on demand and co-sleeping, both of which you embraced, breastfeeding long enough for one baby to say during the night, 'That side's empty. Turn over.'

Sister was really ahead of her time. In the eighties she'd go to the local supermarket and retrieve all the produce that was slightly out of date and distribute it amongst the families she visited. Behind her back, you and your friends thought it hilarious. Going to the bins and getting the out-of-date food! Who would do that? If it was good, you'd use it though, no question. Now you'd call it freecycling, and it's a movement that garners respect for reducing food waste and environmental impact. Who'd have thought you'd have seen it first in your small hometown, back in the day?

Over the years, over the decades, Sister always had a chat if you saw her. And then she'd have a chat with your eldest daughter who worked at the local council, after you'd moved. She loved to tell her about when she used to visit her with her little baby, confusing her with you.

'I *am* the baby, Sister,' your daughter would say, in her thirties now.

Somewhere along the line, your daughter said it ended up being easier to go along with her and she just answered to Meaghan.

2017

Your daughter last saw Sister recently in the street while visiting home.

'Oh, Meaghan,' she had said to your daughter, confusing her with you again. 'I'll never forget you and your little baby. You were so young, but so confident!

And so clever, all your spice jars lined up in a rack, with labels on them.'

'It's nice to be remembered,' you responded, when your daughter told you.

She loved to remind you how clever you were, what with your labelled spice racks and all.

MUM'S STORY

You know your mother's family stories in a way that comes over time. Almost absorbed by osmosis, the stories have permeated your being, indelibly shaping you. They inform who you are and how you see the world in ways you won't fully understand for a lot of your life. Understandings built over countless hours, sitting around Nan's table in Ouyen; memories shared during long drives or late nights with Mum. Stories imparted, casually, organically as a memory is prompted, a question asked or a gap filled to provide context for another story. Stories not consigned to history, or solely dredged up from the past, but always being layered upon with new chapters. The common thread being a healthy distrust for and wariness of authority, and disdain for the privileged.

You remember one occasion when Pop, old by then, responded outraged when a family member ran afoul of the law and landed in the lock-up overnight. Nothing major, probably drunk in a public place. 'Round up the Boys, Kath,' he proclaimed to your nan. 'We'll break him out.'

Your mum would tell you how, when she was young, the Ouyen townsfolk used to say her family, of distant Irish ancestry, were 'like the Italians' because they always went 'up the street' in a group. This comparison, all at once classist and racist, paints as accurate a picture of Australian country town life as any, you think.

Your grandparents were from farming families. Not the kind of farmers, you know, that occupied a higher class in the community. (Not the kind of farmers you recognise in your own hometown, with land as big as a European country, who drive Land Cruisers and join the local tennis club with team names like 'Wheat and Sheep' or 'Stock and Land'.) Smaller-scale farmers, ninety or so acres.

Your great-grandmother was by all accounts a woman ahead of her time and considered an eccentric. She could fire a gun, always carried a bottle of brandy 'for medicinal purposes' and only allowed a few acres of the farm to be cleared for planting because, she is quoted as saying, 'Nothing good can come from cutting down all the trees.' Not a common thought amongst farmers in the early 1900s.

'The Farm' at Bronzewing near Ouyen still holds almost mythical connotations in your extended family despite (or maybe because of?) no one having lived there for over half a century. Family far and wide feel an almost spiritual connection to the place. Stories abound within the family and you're not the first cousin to write about it.

When your grandparents married in the 1930s, there was still a divide between their respective Catholic and Protestant faiths. Pop was a farmer, rabbit trapper and expert horseman. He was as handsome as a movie star and a character larger than life.

It's hard now to imagine religion being such a divider in Australia. And yet it was in Mum's lifetime. Enough for her and her siblings to be followed home from school by the Catholic priest while Pop was away in the army during the Second World War. An ominous figure in his black robes, he'd shout to the four kids, 'You're going to Hell! Your parents aren't really married, they are living in sin!' He apparently arrived on Nan's doorstep one day to harangue her, the so-called lapsed Catholic, to find Pop home on leave. The religious persecution ceased that day. The priest was sent on his way by Pop with a foot up the ass, so the story goes.

Nan was the backbone of the household who raised first her siblings after her mother's death, then her own seven kids, and then several grandkids. Her quiet strength was what held the family together.

Apparently, when she was young, she could ride as well as any of the men. You like to imagine Nan then, outside the kitchen, the house, young and free.

You know now, it wasn't always easy for Nan, being married to the larger-than-life character who loved a drink and a fight and looked like a film star.

There's a spot near The Farm that was locally known as 'Blackfella's Hill', and Pop would tell how, before his time even, Aboriginal people used to gather there from far and wide. Fires lit up the whole area, he would say. Earth thick with ash from countless fires over years, maybe centuries. Maybe from Time Immemorial.

In the 1970s, your mum advised the newly formed Aboriginal Cooperative in Robinvale, located an hour from Ouyen, of Blackfella's Hill. The 1970s was a time of rapid social change and action in Australia, and for the first time, Aboriginal self-determination was being considered. Mum thought the area should be preserved, recognised as a Sacred Site.

The newly appointed Aboriginal cultural officer came to Ouyen and Pop took him to the Hill. Soon after, Parks Victoria fenced off Blackfella's Hill to protect it. Mum didn't think the local farmers would have been pleased about that, which was an added bonus.

You've grown up with this story, you have been to this place, with Mum. The thought of this lost history is staggering. You can almost see the fires lighting up the dark bush, the stars hanging low above, as you wonder about the Ceremony of Blackfella's Hill.

Nan and Pop's home was the last house at the end of a dusty red dirt and stone track lined with a dozen or so houses, surrounded by rough Mallee scrub. Dust and heat and flies that stuck to kids' noses. Somewhat at odds with the harsh, dry landscape, the area had the enchanted name of Fairy Dell. Your mum told how a neighbour, when he'd had too much to drink (which was always), would proclaim, 'Fairy Dell? More like Fairly Bloody Hell!'

And yet it did have a touch of magic to it, the house in Fairy Dell. Really just a cabin clad in iron built by Pop. Pretty rough and basic, and cobbled together as the family grew.

You hold fond memories of Christmas in great numbers where Nan, despite the heat, would churn out a roast Christmas dinner and her famous trifle. Lots of laughing, kids playing, and at least one uncle facedown in the dust after a few too many beers. Maybe a punch-up.

You know there was always a meal at their table, no matter how little they had, for anyone who needed one. Generous to a fault, story has it Pop would kill a pig and promise a leg to twenty-one of his closest mates.

As kids, you played in the scrubby bush, picking paper daisies and making cubbies out of snottygobble, the green, stringy, sticky weed that grew profusely. You'll never forget the shock of seeing the genus on a nature TV show sometime in the 1980s. 'Cassytha pubescens, commonly known as snottygobble,' the narrator said, catching your ear as an image of snottygobble flashed on the screen. You'd thought it was a made-up Ouyen name.

Later, with your own kids, you would sit around Nan's kitchen table when you would visit with Mum. There was special excitement when Mum's groovy young sister, Bub, would come. She would regale you all with her stories while you sat around the table drinking coffee, Pop drinking sweet sherry and water, a 'cool drink', he'd call it, smoking tobacco. You were all sad when they changed the name of Fairy Dell to the more pedestrian Lawler Street.

Your mum was a teacher and a working mother at a time when, in your world, not that many were. You can still see in her the clever, spirited girl she must have been—despite in grade 6 a teacher telling her, 'You're not really intelligent, you just have a photographic memory.' She worked on weekends from the age of twelve at the Fairy Dell Café and at Joe Walsh's Store on school holidays. After finishing high school, she took herself off to Ballarat Teachers' College.

Ballarat was a city of fifty thousand then, famous for the 1850s gold rush that saw it gain international attention and a flood of immigration due to the rich gold deposits. It's located just under four-hundred kilometres from Ouyen; you imagine it must have felt further away in the 1950s on the long train ride. It's never been said, but you've always known that for Mum, going to Teachers' College was no mean feat, at that time, from that place.

How different life at Teachers' College must have been from home in Fairy Dell. Mum tells you of the time she was summoned by the college head, the 'Dreaded Tommy Turner'. The hostel superintendent had made a complaint, and the head told your mum she would have to find private accommodation, could no longer board in the College hostel. Her crime, punishable by eviction? She had tied up her bedroom curtains, which fronted the main street, in knots. *'We don't do that here,'* the head had admonished. Apparently, tying up one's curtains was a 'low class' thing to do.

'I told him,' Mum remembers, 'I would have to leave Teachers' College then and go home, as no one in my small town will believe I was kicked out of the hostel over such a trivial thing.'

You can picture it now, the young country girl squarely facing off the head. She didn't back down then, and she's never backed down since. Mum wasn't kicked out and finished her teacher's training with no further incident.

There's a photo of Mum on her last day at Old Ballarat Teachers' College taken in December 1955, posing, laughing, holding her books. It looks so natural and spontaneous, and she so happy. As though the photographer had just caught the moment as she departed, clutching her books.

'I love this photo,' you say.

Mum tells you, 'We set it up. My friends and I marched out one after the other, all stood in the same place, holding the same books, for the photo.'

You love it even more.

THERE BUT FOR THE GRACE OF GOD?

Robinvale 1990s

You were at a local Charity Society meeting, a secular not-for-profit organisation that had been providing assistance to those in need in Australia for over a century. In your town, at this time, assistance was primarily given in the form of food or petrol vouchers, a night's accommodation in an emergency, or basic clothing or homewares. Along with you, a family aide worker at the local Aboriginal Cooperative, there were representatives from different churches and local government.

Many on the committee were hypervigilant, on high alert to the possibility of those who may be 'abusing' the system. To your way of thinking, most people who availed themselves of the service were doing it tough. Yes, there might have been issues with gambling, substance misuse or other challenges, but those were the symptom of bigger, more entrenched structural issues of disadvantage. Walking the gauntlet for a ten-dollar food voucher and then fronting up to the only supermarket in town with it clearly marked *Charity Society Food Voucher* must have been hard, and not something most people were keen to do unless desperate, in your experience.

You wondered about the motives of those who had such little faith in humanity, so quick to judge, so pious in their giving. The arbiters of the deserving and non-deserving. Not all—not your dear friend, the Uniting Church minister who had had whole families sleeping on his lounge room floor for weeks when they had no place to go—but some. Too many.

Your attention returned to the conversation, where they were discussing who should be distributing the vouchers and how to put limitations on the times the public can come and request one.

'Because,' noted one reverend, 'my wife is often interrupted at all times of the day! Someone even came looking for a food voucher and interrupted our Christmas dinner !'

The irony of this statement was lost on most of the committee. Sadly.

Mildura 2000s

It was October, which meant Mildura Show time.

The show is an institution that draws crowds from around the district. A spectacle of flashing lights, rides, showbags. A huge Ferris wheel can be seen across the town, with it all culminating with a fireworks display on the final night.

You were in your new role at the local non-government organisation that provides a range of services to families in need of support. Some of your colleagues were discussing the Mildura Show and forecasting the repercussions they would see with their 'clients' the following week, predicting they would spend all their money at the Show.

'Well,' one of them said, 'someone from the Salvation Army told me that at Christmas they won't deliver food hampers to families if there is a pay TV satellite dish on the roof. They say if they can afford that, they don't need a hamper.'

Nods of approval around the table.

Because God forbid poor people should have some enjoyment, take their kids to the show or watch pay TV.

'I'll probably blow my budget too, to take the kids to the show,' was all you said and you left them to it.

Struggle Street, Australian national television 2015

_____

You had been following the build-up of the upcoming three-part series *Struggle Street*. The broadcaster, SBS, promoted the series—filmed over a six-month period— as an 'observational documentary' that went beyond the tabloid headlines and into the lives of some of the most under-resourced communities in Mount Druitt, Western Sydney. It touted the series as one that explored issues of disadvantage, but also triumph and joy despite overwhelming odds.

This was not how the community or the participants received the completed series. Accusations of sensationalism, misrepresentation and a negative focus on the suburb abounded. Labelling the series as 'poverty porn', the Mayor of Blacktown threatened to surround SBS headquarters with garbage trucks.

It is a hard series to watch. Poverty, fights, drugs, child protection, homelessness. Yes, it's all there.

Your daughter texted you while you were watching. *Are you watching Struggle Street?*

Yes, you responded.

I feel like crying, I know these people.

I know. Me too.

What you both felt was that everyone is more than their struggles. Everyone is more than their problems or their circumstances.

Yes, *Struggle Street* shone a light on an area of Sydney the more affluent suburbs would rather ignore. *What next, though?* you wondered.

Q+A, Australian national television 2016

You were watching *Q+A*, the current affairs panel show on the ABC, the national broadcaster, that hosts a variety of politicians and commentators. It takes questions from the audience and encourages vigorous debate.

It's had its fair share of controversy and newsworthy TV moments. In 2010, an audience member threw his shoes at then Prime Minister John Howard in protest to Australia's involvement in the war in Iraq.

In this episode, an audience member named Duncan was asking the panel, including the assistant treasurer Kelly O'Dwyer, a question around tax changes announced in the recent national budget.

Duncan told the audience and the panel that he had a 'low education', lived on a disability pension, and sometimes drove trucks. He made the point that lifting the tax-free threshold would be life changing for him, whereas for the 'rich people' it would be hardly noticed. Duncan posed the question: why didn't he get the tax cut, but rather the wealthy did?

Duncan's question was spot on, and it spoke to the experience of many struggling unemployed and underemployed people. It immediately struck a chord, with tweets rolling across the TV screen supporting Duncan. Momentum built and Duncan was immediately swept up as the 'poster boy of the left'. A GoFundMe donation page called 'Buy Duncan Storrar a Toaster' was set up on his behalf, stating:

> Hey - Duncan seems like a good bloke
> and a little bit of cash goes a long way. We
> reckon he deserves a bit of a helping hand
> so we've decided to buy him a new toaster.
> 6 grand oughtta cover it. And if he has a
> little bit left over, maybe he can take his kids
> to the movies or something.
> Would you like to kick in a few dollars?

And kick in Australia did, raising over sixty thousand dollars on Duncan's behalf.

'Watch them come after the poor bastard now,' you commented to your husband.

And come after him they did. 'They' being the right-wing media, who—despite being informed by Duncan of his mental health concerns—dug deep into his past to discredit, humiliate and paint Duncan as an undeserving recipient of the country's (unasked for) generosity. Which, by the way, he set aside for his kids' education and needs, and made donations to very worthy causes—one being the men's shed where he hid from the media storm that had ensued.

You posted on social media soon after: 'Hands up, who wants to ask a question on *Q+A*?'

University lecture 2019

You were running a tutorial in a social policy class. The social work students had just watched a series of interviews where people shared their stories of being recipients of government welfare benefits.

One student offered their critique of the exercise: 'I don't think this is actually a reflection of people on welfare. These are more people who things have happened to ... there are reasons they are on welfare.'

'Yes,' you replied. 'That's right. That's actually everyone receiving a benefit.' There is no 'Other'.

ON FAITH

1990s

The church's fete was in full swing. It had pretty much had the same format for decades. Cake stalls, homegrown produce for sale, a barbecue, lucky dip and spinning wheels. Maybe a jumping castle. Fairly staid. More recently however, the large Pacific Islander community who had settled in the town from the late seventies onward really changed the face of the fete. Overwhelmingly observant Christians, the Pacific Islander community formed large congregations within each of the established faiths, and had formed their own churches as well.

The performances of singing and dancing the Tongan congregation gave were awe-inspiring. Vocal harmonies that sent chills down your spine. The energy and pageantry of traditional dance like fireworks going off in the rather bland landscape of scones and homegrown squash for sale. Men and women, girls and boys adorned in traditional dress, grass and mat skirts, shells, feathers and flowers. Fierce and proud. Their bodies gleaming, oiled for the crowd to adorn them with money.

The performances were spectacular. And a spectacular fundraiser. Large amounts of money were raised as onlookers stuck a fifty- or twenty-dollar note onto a dancer. All going to the church. The small amounts usually raised at the fete paled into insignificance at the collection gathered by the Tongan dancers.

Until the new minister said, 'No more.'

The dancing and singing he loved and appreciated, encouraged and supported. But no more raising money by dancing.

When you asked him why he stopped the very traditional practice of sticking money on the dancers, he replied, 'You don't see any white people sticking money on. It all comes from the Pacific Islander community, beyond what they can afford, and it's exploiting them in the name of the church.'

You often think of your dear friend, the new minister

who was not frightened to make a stand on this issue, who could see first-hand the pressure this placed on the Pacific Islander community and called it out.

The church may have been poorer, but the town richer for actions such as this.

2010s

_____

You have always thought the Anglos have a long way to go when it comes to ritual and community in the face of Death.

When you think of an Anglo funeral, it's usually over in a few hours—a wake that may or may not have alcohol to help lubricate the grieving process, and not much else. That's not to say privately, within families, extended families and community groups, there aren't a range of emotional and physical supports. On the contrary, country people are renowned for coming out to help their neighbours in need.

But for sheer scale of production, community involvement and ritual, you have long admired the Pacific Islander traditions you've observed in your town.

Like any outsider's view, yours is flawed and probably romanticised, but it all seems so healthy to you, the embracing of the rituals around death. Prayers that continue for days, culminating in an all-night vigil. The body of the deceased is on display and anointed with perfume and oil by a family member charged with this duty. Children come and go; they might fall asleep amongst those praying but are not shielded, rather held up close and personal to Death as a part of Life.

As part of the ritual, food is prepared in vast quantities and distributed to the community.

Upon leaving the church after paying your respects at one such vigil, you were confronted by the sight of a huge car trailer completely full of polystyrene takeaway boxes packed with homemade food, prepared by the family to distribute to those, like you, paying their respects. Pork and cassava, potato and noodles, handed out with hundreds of poppers or Tetra Paks of juice with a straw.

You were given a takeaway container, a popper and a bag containing (what felt like) several kilos of raw beef. A cow had been killed and the meat was being distributed amongst the mourners.

'Don't give me any,' you protested. 'Keep it for others.'

'No.' They corrected you. 'You must take it. It is what you do.'

You stood corrected and gratefully accepted the proffered food.

Pigs had been killed and cooked, young men had sat up all night in their family's backyards, turning the sticks impaling full pigs over fires kept smouldering. Pots of food were prepared and served by young women. Everyone had a place. Everyone had a job to do. Everyone was grieving together.

You were told the family members had hardly slept in days, so busy they had been with the funeral rites being observed. The next steps were explained to you. 'Next, they will dig the grave, then after the burial they will sleep for a few days.'

The day of the funeral, the grave had been dug by the sons and other family members. The community has assembled. Tongan men and women wrapped in traditional woven ta'ovala mats, some wrapped right up to their necks. Young people in their Adidas clothes and traditional ta'ovala. Those closest wearing a T-shirt with the image of the departed on it—their mother, grandmother, sister or aunt. Rituals old and new. Christian prayers and traditional customs. Equally revered.

The comfort of ritual and togetherness, sharing the preparing and eating of food, hard physical work preparing the grave and then, the sleep of the exhausted.

ASSIMILATION'S LAST GASPS

You've always been uncomfortable with the name 'Save the Children Fund', as in the worldwide charity. *Save them from what?* you would wonder. Poverty, the Fund would say. Lack of opportunity, it would say. *With disregard of their culture,* you would think. Assimilationists in preschool teachers' clothing, you've long felt.

The Save the Children Fund was introduced to Australia in 1951 and set up shop in your small hometown a few years later, stating their priority in Victoria was to provide preschool services for 'Aboriginal Australians as well as disadvantaged non-Aboriginal children'.

It had been a fixture in your hometown, the Save the Children Preschool, long before your time. Many people would rave about the 'good works' it did. Many still do.

You can see that for mums, often juggling lots of

kids with not many resources, the relief of the Save the Children bus pulling up to take the kids for half a day must have been great. Or the provision of a school lunch when there wasn't much help for struggling families.

The need was there and still is, you don't dispute that. It was the saviour philosophy and parochial attitude they clutched to that you struggled with.

In times past, the 'good works' included 'homemaking' classes for Aboriginal women. Your good friend who attended as a young mother told you how they used to run sewing and cooking classes. We know that this had been part of the wider assimilation policies of the 1960s and our hometown was one of the chosen sites. Your friend showed you photos from the 1950s of a Christmas party at the Save the Children Fund hall—rows of Aboriginal kids 'all shined up', as she put it. One with a big white bow in her hair. A priest was handing out bottles of Coca-Cola.

'They dressed us up like that for the photos,' she said. 'Stuck the bow on our head too.'

You also knew the Aboriginal community as resilient and resourceful. Elders would tell you how they would go to the Save the Children Fund Centre; it was an outing, they could utilise the services offered in hard times. You know now that there is always more than one story, and stories from times of oppression are often intertwined with stories of survival, success and community.

The kinder remained a fixture over the decades, thankfully with more Aboriginal control. Your own kids attended. Dreamtime storybooks were told at story time. Aboriginal stories. Legends. Oral Histories passed down through generations, beautifully written and illustrated. The teacher would type up and paste her own words over the stories in the Dreamtime books, so used to being the Voice of Authority, so unable to give that up. This very action saying, *I can tell this story, your stories, better than you.*

Finally, during the late 1990s, the local Aboriginal organisation officially took full control of the kinder. It was no longer called Save the Children Preschool. The Assimilationists had trouble letting that go and lobbied that the name should remain 'Save the Children' for historical reasons. The Board of Directors at the Aboriginal organisation disagreed, and thankfully the name was changed, and the last vestige of the assimilationist policies was shed. It seemed.

You became aware in the early 2000s that there was a box kept there with the family details of everyone in the Aboriginal community documented on index cards. Not a preschool enrolment procedure, more like a Mission register or an anthropological study. You and your friend went to check. You worked for the organisation and your friend was a Board member, so you could do that.

You asked to see the box. The teacher told you it was her predecessor's record keeping, but reluctantly showed you. A grey-steel box with Aboriginal families each allocated a card. Information included when babies were born, parents' names, details, marriages, divorces. People's lives, your life, your children, your divorce, all captured and cross-referenced in this grey box because the Assimilationist felt it their right to do so.

You were incensed.

You took the card with your name and tore it up.

Nearly twenty years later, your only regret is that you didn't take the whole box.

SUICIDE

Suicide. You remember the first time it crashed into your world.

Of course, you knew about it, had read about it. Some vague discussion overheard as a kid about a friend of your cousin. Sad experiences, discussed in hushed tones.

You were visiting your nan as a child at Ballarat Hospital and outside the window, shards of glass fell, followed by the shape of a man. He looked like he was flying. How people look just before the parachute pops open. Well, that's how it looked to your eight-year-old self. But there was no parachute.

Your mum slammed your head into the hospital bed, but you'd already seen him sail past the window.

Your mum told you it was an accident and he was fine, he'd landed on the awning.

You'd not doubted that story, that he'd survived,

until only a few years ago when you asked about it and Mum told you he had in fact hit the pavement and died, having jumped from the second storey. The memory feels vivid and unreal in equal measure.

But the first time suicide really hit your consciousness, it hit hard. It came crashing into your home and your world, and its malevolent presence hasn't really left. Hanging around like an unwelcome guest.

A mother screaming. A call for help at the front door. Your partner was rushing across the road. All the wails and cries and sirens of tragedy. You stayed inside and tried to keep the kids distracted.

Your partner came back later, ashen-faced and shaking.

A young man, a teenager, had taken his life.

Your partner told you he had released him and laid him down as best he could. He told you he had got into trouble with the police for cutting the young man down. Apparently, he shouldn't have.

'I couldn't leave him like that,' he told you. 'For his mother's sake.'

Years later, you were sitting in the local bowling club while yet another young man's family said goodbye to their son and brother who had taken his life. Shock permeated the air like electricity. You could feel it almost physically sting your cheeks.

The air was hard to breathe, such was the weight of anguish in the room.

You remember they played 'Boys from the Bush' by Lee Kernaghan.

We're the boys from the bush and we're back in town
We get high when the sun goes down
We're life members of the Outback Club
We're the boys from the bush come in from the scrub

The last time you had sat in that room at the bowling club listening to this song, kids from the local primary school were linedancing to it at their end-of-year performance. Little kids with wide gap-tooth smiles in flannelette shirts and too-big cowboy hats.

That's what should be happening, you thought, to this song. Dancing. Celebrating.

Not this poor family sending off their son.

You got a call at work. A young woman, a young mother

had taken her life. You knew this woman; you were teenagers together.

'Can you go and tell her aunty?' they asked you.

You drove to her aunty's house, and sat on her sofa. You could hear kids and family life going on in the other rooms.

You told her, as gently and as clearly as you could, what had happened.

She stared blankly at you.

'No,' she said firmly. 'No.'

'I'm so sorry,' you said.

'No,' she said, imploring you. 'Please don't tell me this. Please. Don't tell me this.'

As if you could take it back, make it not true.

You wished you could take it back. You wished you could make it not true.

You asked her if her husband was home. Suddenly, it was like a spell had broken. She screamed to her husband what had happened and grief and pain seemed to engulf her. Her husband picked her up, holding her as she screamed. You felt like an intruder in that moment of raw grief and slipped out the door.

You could hear her wailing as you got into the car,

shaking.

Another funeral. And another. And another. Young men lined up. Pallbearers. Dressed in matching T-shirts, printed with the image of their departed brother or sister, cousin or friend, when they were smiling. When they were alive. Like a rockstar T-shirt, issued for their final performance. Wearing their T-shirt of love and loss. Wearing their new uniform of Grief. Flanking the coffin like modern-day Warriors.

This reimagined ritual took your breath away.

It hangs there always, the fear of suicide. Crouching just out of reach. You can see it out of the corner of your eye. Hiding amongst every occasion, happy or sad. It doesn't mind which, it'll hang on the edge of complacence, reminding you it's there.

You know that the suicide of a close friend or family member places young people immediately in a high-risk category. You know you need to talk honestly about it.

You know. You know. You know. You know. YOU KNOW.

You feel as though you have to physically fight it off, hold it at bay by sheer force of will or it will find you.

You call your young people incessantly, obsessively.

Are you OK? Are they OK?

IS EVERYONE OK?

It became normal, upon hearing of the death of a young person, to hope fervently that it was a car accident. Or cancer. Or some other medical emergency. It becomes normal.

Such is the damage you know suicide brings.

2021

Your daughter was attending Aboriginal cultural competence training at her new job, shadowing her colleague, who was presenting. They were the only two Aboriginal people in the room.

Her colleague presented the statistics. They are stark and they are confronting. Aboriginal people in Australia are many times more likely to die by suicide than non-Aboriginal people.

A person in the group challenged the statistic, saying she had just googled it and that suicide wasn't higher at all in the Aboriginal community!

She had just googled it? She had just googled it.

Your daughter was stunned. There was a pause.

Your daughter spoke.

'Whatever you have found on Wikipedia, I can tell you this. I have personally lost more family and community members to suicide than I can count on my hands and my feet.'

Silence.

It's hard to hear about?

Imagine living it.

ALLIES:
IT'S NOT
ABOUT US

Recent events nationally and internationally have brought the media spotlight back to the abject failure of Australia as a nation towards our First Peoples. You say 'media spotlight' as we know that for Aboriginal and Torres Strait Islander Peoples, this lived reality of genocide and ongoing colonialism hasn't gone anywhere, and the fight is an everyday reality. You say 'back to' as we know that it doesn't take much to push any examination of the inequality faced by Aboriginal and Torres Strait Islander Peoples off the front page of mainstream media.

White Australians have the privilege of choice regarding when and if they engage with activism or action around issues impacting Aboriginal and Torres Strait Islander Peoples. Indigenous Peoples do not. It is literally Every day. It is literally Life and Death. It is unrelenting.

Recently some white Australians and some young people have been made more aware of Australia's ongoing shame of Aboriginal deaths in custody. This is not a phenomenon recently 'discovered'. Thirty years ago on 15 April 1991, the Royal Commission into Aboriginal Deaths in Custody was tabled. Three hundred and thirty-nine recommendations were handed down, most of which have been ignored. Tragically, at least four hundred and seventy-five Aboriginal People have died in custody since then.

Whatever the path, Allies, let's stay the distance. Let's ensure our support and activism is authentic, targeted, and directed by Aboriginal and Torres Strait Islander Peoples.

Let's take it beyond the comfort zone.

Let's do no harm.

You think about the recent negative furore around a Sydney public school's Harmony Day activity where year 5/6 students made Black Lives Matter activism posters. Some were pointed at police injustices.

The right-wing media, typically, went wild.

Aboriginal teacher and actor Luke Pearson rightly

pointed out that in this country ten-year-old children can be jailed, so should therefore be entitled to opinions. We also know the vast majority of, if not all, incarcerated children are Indigenous.

You commend any teacher for opening up the space for complex and hard conversations. To foster awareness and a critical view among young people is important. You would wonder though, as Allies, are we seeking guidance from Aboriginal and Torres Strait Islander Peoples about how we can support the cause? How we can best contribute? How we can take the learnings beyond a feel-good activism moment? How we can ensure our own endeavours don't Make it About Us and detract from the core issues?

The mainstream media, well versed in the deficit reporting of Aboriginal and Torres Strait Islander experiences, again, made this an issue of othering and fear. The media have made this about the school, the teacher, and allegations of 'brainwashing' students.

This ended up being a handy moment for Whitewashing for the government and mainstream media, which will likely result in further marginalisation of Aboriginal and Torres Strait Islander perspectives within the public school system. You would suggest this was unfortunately enabled by well-meaning activism.

Allies, it's not about us.

THE PRIVILEGE IN SHARING 'PARENTING FAILS'

In this age of the open platform of social media, there has been increasing online commentary from parents, mainly women, sharing with honesty their daily struggles and challenges in parenting, often in a lighthearted, self-deprecating way. These stories are a welcome move away from the idea of an 'Instagram perfect' presentation of mother as 'superwoman' that has prevailed.

The idea of this 'ideal' of motherhood is not new and nor is the pressure for mothers to present a socially acceptable exterior, regardless of how they are really coping. Social media has, however, publicly ramped up the scrutiny. The pushback from women against the 'perfect mother' image comes from a good place. The idea of disrupting this one-dimensional persona can be seen as a strike for feminism. The portrayal of 'less than perfect' parenting and women sharing complex and multifaceted lives beyond a Stepford wife trope is important and relevant.

Many well-known media personalities, writers and bloggers share their 'parenting fails' in this manner, often with comedic effect. The stories and pictures women share depicting children falling asleep on the floor while they struggle to meet a deadline, the serving of two-minute noodles, or being called by the school because they've missed school pick-up are realities that many parents can identify with, and have experienced. The honesty of these 'everywoman' stories can serve to take the pressure off those trying to 'do it all' by showing no one is alone in this struggle.

And yet, these stories always make you feel deeply frustrated and annoyed. Furious, even.

Do they not know how privileged a position they are in to be able to joke about this stuff? Are they so arrogantly unaware of that privilege, so lacking in insight? you wonder. Often unkindly.

You know we are all informed by our world view and you know you view these snapshots of life from across a cultural and class divide. There is no doubt that factors such as class, ethnicity and socio-economic and career status provide a safe launching pad for self-deprecating humour such as these 'parenting fails'.

Let's pause for a moment, though, and consider the same scenarios through a different lens.

Imagine the same witty commentary around pouring a glass of wine at 5 pm at the end of a challenging day of at-home learning while giving the kids cereal for dinner again, without the buffer of social acceptance and an unquestioned belief in your societal safety as a parent.

Imagine this scenario being shared by a very young parent, or one struggling with mental health challenges who has been 'flagged' by child-protection services.

What if the onus is on you to prove you are able to parent safely, that you are worthy to parent?

Oh, and child-protection services check social media too. Just saying.

Or what if you are a foster parent who is under the important but constant scrutiny of departmental workers to prove you are providing 'good-enough care' for the children you are caring for under guardianship of the State?

What if the humorous video shared isn't set in a comfortable middle-class home, but rather cramped public housing, shared accommodation or a caravan? Is it as funny if you are feeding the kids two-minute noodles again because that's all you can afford? What if the deadline you have to meet is reporting to Centrelink so they don't cut your payments off? What if the chance at any job, much less a career to struggle with, might feel as out of reach as a trip to the moon?

How might it feel telling your social worker, whose job it is to ensure you are meeting the required standards of care, that you missed school pick-up because you were so overwhelmed you forgot? Not humorous or judgement-free in that context. Actually, try to imagine having to report to a social worker at all.

What if you are an Aboriginal or Torres Strait Islander parent, whose living memory knows the reality of children being forcibly removed from their families and communities, based only on their Aboriginality. 'Parenting fails' may not be a laughing matter in this context.

How might it feel if you've never been on a holiday to a resort, watching an 'everywoman' joke on social media about the exhaustion of parenting on holidays because it is So Much More Work!

You have seen it around you in your own privileged environment. A parent sent a WhatsApp message to the class advising that their child had head lice. Socially responsible, yes. You applauded that in theory. But in reality, you were stunned.

You told your husband, 'We'd have died before we did that back home, for fear of being judged!'

Don't scratch at school, kids were told, they might think you have nits. Actually, you probably wouldn't do it now if you were honest. Such is the weight of knowing what it is to be stereotyped.

You liken your frustration at this trend to the critique of second-wave feminism being a white middle-class woman's concern. That it wasn't inclusive of black and brown women. Women of colour. Culturally diverse women. Poor women.

It's a critique you agree with. Your own mother didn't have time to join a feminist movement in the sixties and seventies. She was too busy working. She was too busy fighting. She was too busy being one.

You think about the now-iconic feminist statement, 'My feminism will be intersectional or it will be bullshit,' taken from the article of the same name written by

Flavia Dzodan in 2011. Dzodan has written extensively about how it has felt to see her words taken out of context, appropriated, watered down, and used without permission or recognition. You can buy all manner of merchandise depicting those words now. Sometimes it credits Dzodan. Sometimes not. Sometimes her name is spelled incorrectly. She profits from none of it.

Is that what we want, you wonder, *in society?* Bite size, feel-good slogans? A badge to wear? Is that what this is? A safe, socially acceptable 'challenge' to the pressures society places on women in a witty humblebrag?

Does that negate its value? you wonder.

Let's continue to share the trials and tribulations of juggling career and parenting with honesty and humour. Let's continue to highlight the often-unattainable standards placed on women, and especially in these challenging times. But let's take this further. Let's examine the classist, colonialist, racist structures that prevail.

Let's be honest in our examination and not for a minute pretend that this platform of witty honesty is open to all. Let's acknowledge that this sharing of 'parenting fails' is an example of the bigger issue of protection from societal judgement that only the narrow world of privilege offers.

SYNCHRONICITY

You'd come in to uni on your day off with your five-month-old baby in tow. It was 13 February 2008, and Prime Minister Kevin Rudd was about to make his formal Apology to the Stolen Generations. A momentous, long-awaited occasion. More keenly anticipated as for the past eleven years the former Prime Minister John Howard had refused to make the Apology, despite it being one of fifty-four recommendations handed down in the 1997 Bringing them Home Report into the forced removal of Aboriginal and Torres Strait Islander Children from their Families and Communities.

It was a significant-enough occasion that the university where you worked had opened up a space and would be screening the Apology for anyone in the community who wished to watch.

You headed to the campus and found the room. Surprisingly, there was only one other person in attendance. More surprisingly, it was your former partner and the father of your three Big Kids, the youngest of whom was sixteen.

He didn't even work at the uni, but for another government department.

You greeted each other.

'They told us at work we could come and watch the apology,' he said.

You both commented that you had thought more people would come to watch.

You weren't on bad terms; it'd been over a decade since you both re-partnered. What was it James Taylor had said about he and Carly Simon? 'We don't hang out.' That pretty much summed it up for you too.

It was the first time he'd seen your new baby. He reached out and took her into his arms and nursed and rocked her while you stood in companionable silence, watching the Apology.

It was powerful and moving. Seeing the reaction of the survivors of the Stolen Generations in the Parliament and those gathered outside was emotional.

As you watched, tears slid down your cheeks. You cried for those who were Stolen. You cried for the

Apology. For those who had fought for it, and for those who hadn't lived to see it.

You cried for you both too, standing there together.

2021

You were in a hotel room, writing this essay. Thinking about this experience and wondering how much weight to place on it. Was it as synchronistic as it had felt at the time that only you two had come that day? What were the chances of that? Pretty slim, you thought.

As you were writing this passage, you were crying again. You weren't quite sure why. Nostalgia?

Your mobile rang.

It was not a number you recognised, so you answered in case something was wrong at home.

It was a very earnest girl from Amnesty International. She was following up on the order you had placed some time ago for their free resource on being an Ally alongside Aboriginal and Torres Strait Islander Peoples. You'd ordered it to use with your social-work students.

Because you were in tears, you couldn't interject fast

enough to cut off the conversation graciously.

The earnest young woman took the opportunity to give you the full spiel on How to be a Good Ally. She was very passionate and advised you of how much she had learned since doing this training, sharing some of the learnings that she thought might surprise you.

You composed yourself enough to thank her for the call and hang up. Wiping your tears, you decided you did believe in synchronicity.

You were talking to your dear friend a bit later. They knew the Kevin Rudd story. You told them about the Amnesty International addition.

'Oh, Meagh,' they said, 'we don't think of you as an Ally!'

SIS IS TIRED

You were talking with your eldest daughter on the phone. As always, your conversation was diverse and encompassed everything from the family day-to-day, school and work, to the big world events.

You were discussing some issues at the kids' school. The kind of unnecessary hurdles and bumps in the road that needed calling out, needed addressing.

She won this battle. Like the one before. And the one before.

Racism.

Unconscious bias.

White privilege.

White fragility.

Stereotyping.

Navigating a life that is often a battleground is exhausting.

'Sis is tired,' she half joked.

Later you received a text from her:

Sometimes I think life would be easier if I didn't have this fire inside me to always fight for what's right but then I think na fuck it gotta be the change no matter how hard it is.

Sis is Tired. Sis is Tired.

THE REFERENDUM

October 2023

You don't know when you realised your discomfort in discussing the First Nations Voice to Parliament referendum with people, as in 'outsiders', really hit home. A few people, friends and family members asked you, and you were only comfortable in giving a general answer of support but acknowledging alternate Aboriginal Peoples' views.

But really. Who are we, white people, to have a say in this? To make this decision that will have little to no impact on most people's day to day lives, and yet is so profound to many Aboriginal Peoples.

Who are we to say. To assume all Aboriginal Peoples, think, feel and will vote the same. You know many Aboriginal People who are against it, for a range of reasons.

'What about Sovereignty?'

'Why should we take these crumbs?'

'Treaty Now!'

It's not that simple.

Noongar author Claire G Colman, wrote a wonderful piece, 'Why I stand for Yes, and why that's hard to say out loud' which eloquently articulates the struggle of many Aboriginal Peoples in grappling with this.

You feel, as an Ally, validated.

More and more people share their position, acknowledging their respect for the Black Sovereign movement, yet decision to vote Yes.

Rapper Briggs sums it up on social media. 'There is no; yes, progressive no, racist no. Just yes and no'.

Your family and friends' discussion is along those lines, landing firmly on Yes. You all decide a No vote is supporting a racist position and it's very possibly Now or Never.

'It's better than nothing,' is the final consensus in your family.

The magnitude of defeat was a shock. The texts from

Aboriginal family and friends summing up the feelings.

'I feel like I've been punched in the guts.'

'Albo fucked this up.'

'I didn't think it would get up, but I didn't think we'd get smashed.'

Aboriginal leaders put out a statement and call for a week silence to grieve the result of the Voice. Mildura, your regional hometown had the highest No in Victoria. Lots of discussions about True Colours and the like ensues.

December 2023

You're at Redfern Oval. Daughters, granddaughter and grandson. Ready for Lani to debut in her first game with the Rabbitohs U/17 Rugby. Stinking hot, you're sheltering under a tree when William spots a pug coming towards us being led by his owner. In true four-year-old confidence he asks, 'Can I pat him?'

'Of course,' says the owner and tells us the pugs name is Floyd.

William and Floyd share a moment, and the adults

do too. Floyd's owner, a youngish (probably) white guy in his YES T-shirt. Shae wearing a hat reppin' Darug nations from another footy match. We stand and chat about Floyd's exploits, share a few minutes of community connection.

Floyd the Pug and YES T-shirt guy walk off and I ask Shae, 'Do you think he stood and chatted longer as a sign of support?'

'100% she replied. 'It was like he wanted to say, "Look at my shirt! I voted YES!"'

And we both agreed.

There was something lovely in that small gesture.

CONCLUSION: DID I TELL YOU I GOT A POSTCARD FROM HELEN GARNER?

When you published your book of memoir-based essays, your dear friend Annie summed up all your hopes and fears in one line. 'No hiding now Meagh.'

She knew of the conflict you felt; wanting to have your stories out there, but to remain somewhat safely in the background. Your desire to share your work, entangled with concern of seeming like a self-promoter, a big noter, of 'blowing your own horn'.

You talk a good game. On International Women's Day you post on social media 'Girls! Don't make yourselves small! Take up all the space', along with a photo of you aged about nine in a crocheted skirt and bolero your Nan made. And yet, you agonise over whether you are taking up more than your share.

You feel humbled and overwhelmed by the response you've had to your stories, from friends and strangers alike. At the launch and few small events people showed up for you in a way that moved you beyond words. Family, friends, colleagues, former students and strangers. You share these events online, with immense gratitude, but always with a twinge of 'is it too much yet?'

You see an online post by UK author Emma Gannon that's been widely shared on this very subject. Clearly aimed at female writers, the author opens with 'I won't be apologising for book promotions'. She speaks of how writers work alone, in private for a long time creating their work, and really want to connect with people. She reminds us how many male authors will talk about their work with pride, and without apology. She finishes with 'permission slip granted, promote your work'. You resolve to do this very thing.

You are attending a Writers Festival, and Helen Garner is speaking. Your husband asks, 'Are you going to try and get a copy of your book to her?'

The suggestion makes sense. The first essay in your book is titled 'With Apologies to Helen Garner and thanks to Elizabeth Gilbert', where you outline the motivation and inspiration that set this collection of essays in motion. You reply that you might try and put a few copies in your bag but you're really thinking *as if*.

You wonder how you could manage to, without encroaching on her space, overstepping or being stalky. You imagine seeing her check into the same hotel and leaving a copy at the desk, with a witty note. That type of safe, slightly removed approach appeals.

You (and several hundred others) sit transfixed as Helen Garner is interviewed in a broad ranging discussion. At one point the interviewer mentions receiving correspondence from readers, and Helen states she loves that. Something along the lines of it being a connection with the reader. This shouldn't surprise you. You've read her work and interviews enough to know she's an avid letter and postcard writer.

This emboldens you. You go back to the hotel and write a card thanking her, and pop it into a book. This remains in your bag another few weeks until you take yourself in hand, look up her agent and send it off.

You are at the letter box, sifting through the junk mail. *A postcard!* You haven't received a postcard for ages. Who could it be from? You examine it. The image of an older woman with grey hair and glasses, enamel dish on her lap peeling vegetables. Behind her a cupboard with a corning ware bowls, several bottles and jug; a saucepan on the wall. Patent shoes on checkerboard flooring. You turn it over, strong blue ink and the odd rain spot, and go straight to the signature on the briefly worded card.

'Helen Garner.'

You hold your breath and read the rest. She thanks you for the copy of *Memories and Elephants*.

'I like your tone and openness, and the brevity of the essays - no hot air.

Congratulations - every good wish.'

No hot air. From the Queen of the pared-back prose. You feel your face flush and an overwhelming sense of relief wash over you. Relief and elation. Helen Garner read your book and you will take those few short lines as approval.

You are not above casually calling a few close friends to drop it in the conversation. They are suitably thrilled.

You tell your publisher and send her a photo of the card. To say she is delighted would be an understatement. In her gentle way she suggests we could share it in some way. You say you don't think so, it's private correspondence and you'd feel uncomfortable using it as promotion. She suggests sensibly that Ms Garner would probably expect you to, or she wouldn't have sent it. She speaks of it as a 'gift'.

You ask your husband what he thinks. Annoyingly, he agrees with you. A part of you had hoped he would try and talk you out of your position, *insist* you share it.

In 2020, Fenella Souter, journalist and editor, wrote an opinion piece in the Sydney Morning Herald titled 'What is it about Helen Garner? One reader's appreciation' where she gushes (her word) about receiving a note from Helen and likens it to a 'nod from the Pope'. Souter states, 'she (Garner) knows the power of Helen Garner and uses it for good'.

Of course she does. You have received a wonderful gift and a conclusion to the story. A gift you are proud and thankful to have received.

Pass me my horn please. Toot Toot.

Acknowledgements

I have immense gratitude to so many people in my life who have shown me love and support. People who have believed in me, encouraged me and supported me. Family and friends who know these stories, lived these stories with me, and supported me to tell these stories.

Mum and Dad, who raised us with a strong foundation and sense of social justice that has been the compass in our lives. I feel lucky to have grown up in Robinvale, in our large, diverse community. I also know that it is because I had you both for parents, I was able to grow up embracing the beauty and diversity.

My brother Mark and sister De, the rockstar couple who were the first readers of *The art of casual racism* and encouraged me to write more. Your support has never wavered, thank you.

My dear friend Annabelle, how we have laughed and cried over the years. You validated my writer's voice the most when I needed it the most.

Andy, my friend, distance means nothing, and our friendship is a constant in my life, as are the lessons I have learned from you.

Natasha, thank you for believing these stories were worth sharing. Thank you for 'getting' my voice. Thank you, Georgia, for the very gentle editing, for getting my Love for Capitalising Big Thoughts. I couldn't have dreamt of a better match than the kind press for

Memories and Elephants.

My kids, Leshae, Cleon, Jackson, Aimai and Zeenie, my grandkids, Grace, Leilani, William, Harper and Baby Leshae. These stories are all of us right here. I am lucky to be your mum and your nan.

Leshae, my daughter, you amaze me in your unrelenting passion and commitment to fighting the Good Fight. Sis may be Tired, but she never gives up. Thank you for letting me share your stories, in real time!

Cyrus. Thank you for being the anchor in our lives. Without you, none of this would have been possible.

January 2024

_____

Since releasing *Memories and Elephants* in December 2021, I have been humbled by the feedback I've received. Family, friends and strangers have reached out to offer support, validation or to let me know the book has moved them in some way. This has meant the world to me.

Katie Clements, who brought *Memories and Elephants* into the Year 12 classroom in my hometown Robinvale and Mildura—thank you for valuing local stories and writers.

I offer my heartfelt thanks to Donata Carrazza who first suggested *Memories and Elephants The Play*. After dropping a few hints, Donata reached for my hand across the table and asked, 'Do you know Fiona Blair?' As my mum would say, 'The penny dropped.'

Fiona Blair—thank you for making this an Old Van Production.

Annabelle. We're not finished yet! I love that three Robinvalians are working on this.

Arts Mildura—thank you for supporting my

hometown story.

Richard Frankland—thank you, my friend. Your personal and professional support has given me the confidence to keep going!

Most of all, thank you to the Big Kids and their father Will who have supported me in taking our stories further.

About the author

Dr Meaghan Katrak Harris is a social worker, academic and writer. She has a long and diverse professional background across the public and private sectors and the arts.

Memories and Elephants: The Art of Casual Racism, Meaghan's first work of creative nonfiction, was released in December 2021, receiving excellent reviews.

Arts Mildura commissioned *Memories and Elephants* for a theatre adaptation, by Fiona Blair of The Old Van Theatre Company, in February 2024.

Also under development is an historical fiction screenplay Two Mile to Town, co-written by Meaghan and her brother Mark Harris, set in small town Australia in the late 1960's set against an historically factual background of the assimilationist policies of the time.